ON TRIAL

A Criminal Trial Simulation
The Case of the Big Bad Wolf

Written by Margaret Schweitzer

Illustrated by Mary Lou Johnson

Prufrock Press Inc.
P.O. Box 8813
Waco, TX 76714-8813
Phone: (800) 998-2208
Fax: (800) 240-0333
http://www.prufrock.com

Common Core State Standards Alignment

Grade Level	Common Core State Standards in ELA-Literacy
Grade 4	RF.4.3 Know and apply grade-level phonics and word analysis skills in decoding words
	RF.4.4 Read with sufficient accuracy and fluency to support comprehension.
	W.4.4 Produce clear and coherent writing in which the development and organization are appropriate to task, purpose, and audience.
	SL.4.1 Engage effectively in a range of collaborative discussions (one-on-one, in groups, and teacher-led) with diverse partners on grade 4 topics and texts, building on others' ideas and expressing their own clearly.
	SL.4.3 Identify the reasons and evidence a speaker provides to support particular points.
	SL.4.4 Report on a topic or text, tell a story, or recount an experience in an organized manner, using appropriate facts and relevant, descriptive details to support main ideas or themes; speak clearly at an understandable pace.
Grade 5	RF.5.3 Know and apply grade-level phonics and word analysis skills in decoding words.
	RF.5.4 Read with sufficient accuracy and fluency to support comprehension.
	W.5.1 Write opinion pieces on topics or texts, supporting a point of view with reasons and information.
	W.5.2 Write informative/explanatory texts to examine a topic and convey ideas and information clearly.
	W.5.4 Produce clear and coherent writing in which the development and organization are appropriate to task, purpose, and audience. (Grade-specific expectations for writing types are defined in standards 1–3 above.)
	SL.5.1 Engage effectively in a range of collaborative discussions (one-on-one, in groups, and teacher-led) with diverse partners on grade 5 topics and texts, building on others' ideas and expressing their own clearly.
	SL.5.3 Summarize the points a speaker makes and explain how each claim is supported by reasons and evidence.
	SL.5.4 Report on a topic or text or present an opinion, sequencing ideas logically and using appropriate facts and relevant, descriptive details to support main ideas or themes; speak clearly at an understandable pace.
Grade 6	RI.6.1 Cite textual evidence to support analysis of what the text says explicitly as well as inferences drawn from the text.
	W.6.1 Write arguments to support claims with clear reasons and relevant evidence.
	W.6.4 Produce clear and coherent writing in which the development, organization, and style are appropriate to task, purpose, and audience. (Grade-specific expectations for writing types are defined in standards 1–3 above.)
	SL.6.1 Engage effectively in a range of collaborative discussions (one-on-one, in groups, and teacher-led) with diverse partners on grade 6 topics, texts, and issues, building on others' ideas and expressing their own clearly.
	SL.6.3 Delineate a speaker's argument and specific claims, distinguishing claims that are supported by reasons and evidence from claims that are not.
	SL.6.4 Present claims and findings, sequencing ideas logically and using pertinent descriptions, facts, and details to accentuate main ideas or themes; use appropriate eye contact, adequate volume, and clear pronunciation.
Grade 6-8	RH.6-8.4 Determine the meaning of words and phrases as they are used in a text, including vocabulary specific to domains related to history/social studies.
	RH.6-8.8 Distinguish among fact, opinion, and reasoned judgment in a text.
	WHST.6-8.3 Write narratives to develop real or imagined experiences or events using effective technique, relevant descriptive details, and well-structured event sequences.
	WHST.6-8.4 Produce clear and coherent writing in which the development, organization, and style are appropriate to task, purpose, and audience. (Grade-specific expectations for writing types are defined in standards 1–3 above.)

Contents

Instructions for the Teacher

You know the story of the Big Bad Wolf and the Three Little Pigs. You know what the wolf did. You know that if the wolf were tried for his crimes, that he would surely be guilty. Well, here's an activity that will shed doubt on your previous convictions. After all the evidence has been presented, you'll question whether the wolf is really guilty or merely a victim of wolf prejudice and circumstantial evidence.

This simulation is designed to guide students in conducting their own, non-scripted trial. The materials provide roles for all of the students in a single class and individualized directions instructing students in the roles they are to learn and then perform in the course of the trial. With the teacher acting as the guide, the students will go through all phases of a criminal trial from the beginning through the verdict. Pretrial and most evidentiary and procedural issues are not included.

Before the trial students will discuss communities and rule-making. Then students will sign up for the roles they will play in the trial. You might choose to assign roles if you decide that there are some roles that are too weighty or difficult for some of the students. These are not scripted roles, but rather are guides for the students to follow during the trial. Some of the roles, such as the lawyer and news reporter, require much more work than the others. Both of these roles require that the students do homework and receive additional guidance during pretrial preparation.

The trial procedure should be taken seriously by the students. Students should be asked to dress in a businesslike manner. The trial judge should be a recognized authority figure (a teacher, principal, or local lawyer or judge).

As in a real trial, lawyers drive the trial by presenting opening statements, calling and questioning witnesses, and giving closing arguments. The witnesses in the trial will answer according to the set of facts they are given for the characters they are portraying. The jury will listen and take notes during the trial, and alone it carries the responsibility for the verdict. A follow-up discussion allows students to discuss their observations and criticisms of the process and to consider how their own trial might relate to real trials.

You can adjust the level of complexity in this simulation in several ways. One way to simplify the project is to have students read only "On Trial," "Trial Procedures," and each student's personal role description sheet, thus eliminating two discussions about communities and the legal system. Eliminating the news reporters and a couple of witnesses can also reduce the number of issues raised. Even a simplified trial project will raise many basic issues in American law.

Concepts Presented

This simulation is designed to demonstrate several principles of American life. The concepts that students should learn of as a result of taking part in the discussions and the trial are:

- We are members of many communities, each of which has rules or laws to guide our behavior to protect and benefit the individuals in the group and the community as a whole.

- We respect the rules of each of the communities of which we are a part. Our respect for these rules is a function of our respect for ourselves as individuals, our respect for the institutions we create and conduct, and our respect for others within our community, on whom we depend.

- Americans traditionally take responsibility for creating and maintaining communities and the communities' institutions.
- American laws and institutions seek to balance individual freedoms and community strength.
- It is interesting, challenging, and fun to work and learn together.
- Inherent in working cooperatively, we listen to each other, think carefully, and speak for our own and each other's benefit.

Procedure

The following is the procedure for staging this trial:

1. Lead students in a discussion of communities and laws using the questions on page 11.

2. Lead students in a discussion of laws and the legal system using the questions on pages 12 and 13.

3. Duplicate and hand out copies of pages 16 and 17 to all students. Introduce the trial by having students read through "On Trial, The Case of the Big Bad Wolf." Discuss any new vocabulary and concepts.

4. Duplicate and hand out copies of pages 18 through 20. Go through the Trial Procedures with students. Make sure that students understand how the trial will be conducted and what each of the roles involves.

5. Assign roles or have students volunteer for roles. You or some other authority figure will play the role of the judge. Use page 10 to keep track of who will play each role.

6. Give each person a description of his or her role. Materials should be handed out according to the chart on page 9. Allow students time to acquaint themselves with the information. The lawyers will need time to prepare their cases and the newspaper reporters will need time to interview people and write a newspaper article.

7. Stage the trial according to the procedures outlined in Trial Procedures.

8. Have the jury deliver the verdict.

9. Newspaper reporters should now write, duplicate and distribute a news article about the trial and its outcome.

10. Have students assess the simulation using the questions on After the Trial (pages 44 and 45). You may either hold a class discussion of these questions or you can duplicate the pages and ask students to write their impressions.

Materials

Use the guidelines on page 9 to determine what information should be given to each participant. Because some of the actors in the simulation are supposed to thwart the efforts or contradict the testimony of others, it is important that each student receive only his or her own materials and that each person keep his or her information confidential. Also, some of the actors have been instructed to not talk to the press. While this makes things more difficult for the press, it is realistic and poses a problem that the press deals with when trying to report fairly and accurately on the legal system. Of course though instructed to keep their information confidential, the students might discuss confidential things with each other. This also happens in real trials and the practice and possible problems it poses is worthy of discussion.

The materials for this simulation include the following:

Materials for the teacher

- Two question sheets to provide a guideline for introductory discussions using the Socratic method
- Sign-up sheet for roles to be played in the trial
- After the Trial discussion guide

Materials for students

- On Trial: The Case of the Big Bad Wolf - background information on the trial
- Vocabulary and Vocabulary Match
- Trial Procedures - the rules for courtroom behavior and procedure
- Individuals' Information Files
- After the Trial - This sheet can be duplicated and distributed to students to complete or it can be used by the teacher alone to guide a final discussion of the trial.

Discussions

There are four discussion sessions that are a part of this simulation. Three of the discussions take place before the trial (Communities and Laws, Laws and the Legal System, and Trial Procedures) and one (After the Trial) follows the trial. One discussion that is held at the beginning of the simulation (Trial Procedures) is a discussion of the trial procedures involved in staging the trial and an explanation of the roles students will play. One discussion (After the Trial) is optional and follows the trial. The questions that are provided for this review of what transpired and how students felt about it can be used for a discussion or can be answered in writing by the individual participants.

Two other discussions (Communities and Laws and Laws and the Legal System) are held before the trial and are designed to get students thinking about how people live in groups and how laws and the legal system facilitate peaceful communal living. The discussion guides for these two discussions are in the traditional American method for teaching law – the Socratic method. The teacher asks questions and poses brief hypotheticals in order to lead students to the answers sought. The beauty of the Socratic

method is that a thread of a correct or fruitful answer can be pulled from virtually every student's answer. This method also requires students to listen carefully and respond to each other. In this way, learning, like law, is a community effort.

Objectives for Discussion Sessions

Following are guidelines for three discussion sessions to be held before beginning the simulation. Each discussion has different goals and presents different concepts.

As a result of taking part in the first discussion on **Communities and Laws**, students should learn to recognize that:

- Communities have and need rules.
- Rules are created to help or protect the members of the community.
- Rules are made by the community members themselves.
- Each person is a part of the community, and he or she is part of creating the community's rules, respecting the rules, and changing the rules if they need to be changed.
- The collective decision-making necessary for the creation of rules, laws and institutions, depends on everyone's positive participation.

As a result of taking part in the second discussion on **Laws and the Legal System** students should learn or recognize that:

- Laws are the rules set up by some of our communities – our towns, states, and country.
- People set up the rules in each of the communities.

- We design laws to protect people from being hurt and to guarantee people's rights.

- People can be hurt by other people who break laws.

- People can be hurt if the trial and court system isn't fair.

- If laws are not fair or the trial system is not fair, we have to change it.

The third discussion precedes the trial simulation and is based on the **Trial Procedures** handout. As a result of taking part in this discussion, participants should understand that:

- We show respect in court.

- We tell the truth in court.

- The defendant is innocent until proven guilty beyond a reasonable doubt.

- The judge is in charge of the court.

- The prosecutors represent the people (the community); the defense lawyers represent the defendant.

Special Notes and Hints

The jury deliberations can take a very long time. It's recommended that the trial be scheduled before a break period, such as lunch or recess, so that the jurors can deliberate over sack lunches or during recess. They should not deliberate in the classroom while the rest of the class is present. The other students will be very interested in the deliberations and will be distracting to the jurors. Ideally, the jury should deliberate until they reach a unanimous verdict. The teacher should probably set a time deadline, however, and give the jury time warnings at an hour and at a half hour before they are required to submit a verdict. If this is done, the jury and class should be told that there is not a time deadline in real trials, but this is something that is being done during the simulation so that the class can learn the verdict and conclude the simulation within a reasonable time frame.

The lawyers will need to do a lot of work to prepare for the trial. Each student who expresses interest in being a lawyer should be told that it will require a great deal of work. The students who act as lawyers should be good readers, as they will have to read all of the files several times. The lawyers will also have to be given time to meet with other lawyers on their team and prepare for the trial. A teacher, aide or volunteer should look over their pretrial work and provide some guidance. The opening and closing statements should be clear and concise. Questions for direct and cross examination should be clear and designed to elicit the desired responses.

Duplication and Distribution Guide

Handout Title	Page Number	Number to Duplicate	Give to
Trial Vocabulary	14	30	all participants (optional)
Vocabulary Match	15	30	all participants (optional)
On Trial	16	30	all participants
Trial Procedures	18	30	all participants
Bailiff's Information	21-22	1	bailiff
Lawyer's Information	23-25	4	2 defense lawyers and 2 prosecution lawyers
Sheriff's Information	26-27	5	4 lawyers and the sheriff
Deputy's Information	28	5	4 lawyers and the deputy
Quarter's Information	29	5	4 lawyers and the witness
Fluff's Information	30	5	4 lawyers and the witness
Quack's Information	31	5	4 lawyers and the witness
Slither's Information	32	5	4 lawyers and the witness
Moo's Information	33	5	4 lawyers and the witness
Little Good Wolf's Information	34-35	5	4 lawyers and the witness
Dr. Bear's Information	36	5	4 lawyers and the witness
Beave's Information	37-38	5	4 lawyers and the witness
Snack's Information	39	5	4 lawyers and the witness
Big Green Wolf's Information	40	5	4 lawyers and the witness
Juror's Instructions	41-42	6-12	all jurors
News Reporters' Information	43	2	news reporters
After the Trial	44-45	30	all participants (optional)

Roles for the Trial

Legal Role	Name	Person Playing the Role
judge	none	teacher or principal
defendant	Big Bad Wolf	teacher, aide, principal or parent
lawyer for the prosecution		
lawyer for the prosecution		
lawyer for the defense		
lawyer for the defense		
juror		
juror		
juror		
juror		
juror		
juror		
witness for the defense 1	Dr. Bear, Big Bad's doctor	
witness for the defense 2	Beave, an expert house builder	
witness for the defense 3	Snack, a pig in the neighborhood	
witness for the defense 4	Little Good Wolf, friend of Big Bad Wolf	
witness for the defense 5	Big Green Wolf, cousin of Big Bad Wolf	
witness for the prosecution 1	Sheriff	
witness for the prosecution 2	the deputy	
witness for the prosecution 3	Quarter, horse - lives next to Ann	
witness for the prosecution 4	Quack, goose - lives next to Bob	
witness for the prosecution 5	Fluff, lamb - lives next to Ann	
witness for the prosecution 6	Slither, snake friend of Ann and Bob	
witness for the prosecution 7	Moo, an expert on wolves	
juror *		
juror *		
juror *		
juror *		
juror *		
juror *		
news reporter *		
news reporter *		

Fill unmarked roles before filling roles marked with *.

Communities and Laws

This discussion outline provides the discussion leader with possible focal threads that lead students to other issues on each point. Many relevant threads can be found in the answers to these and related questions. Only this first discussion session (not other discussion sessions held at a later time) includes possible threads. Suggested guiding questions include:

Q. What is a community?

focal thread: **Communities are groups of people**.

example: a town, neighborhood, family

Q. What is the smallest community to which you belong?

focal thread: **There are many different kinds of communities**.

example: family, neighborhood, classroom, school, religious group, club or group such as scouts or sports team

Q. Can you think of any rules that these different communities have?

focal thread: **Each community has rules.**

Q. Compare some of the rules. Are there some rules that are rules in one group or community and not rules in other groups or communities?

focal thread: **Rules are different for different groups and situations.**

Q. Why are the rules different?

focal thread: **Rules exist to meet the needs or risks of each group or community.**

Ask students to suggest rules that everyone is familiar with (preferably outside school) such as wear a helmet when you ride a bike, don't hit people, or clean up after yourself. Select several of the rules mentioned by the students, write them on the board, and talk about the protection and restriction factors for each, one at a time.

Q. (Picking one rule) Why is this a rule? Why did that rule get started?

focal thread: **Rules are to protect everyone or to give everyone a fair chance.**

Q. How does that rule help you? Does the rule always help you?

focal thread: **Rules help everybody in some ways and limit everybody's freedom in other ways.**

Q. Do you agree with the rule? Is that a good rule?

focal thread: **While people might agree that a rule is good, they might also not like the rule because it restricts their freedom.**

Q. Does everybody follow this rule?

focal thread: **Sometimes not everyone follows a given rule.**

Q. If people don't follow the rule, is it still a rule? Do you feel differently about the rule?

focal thread: **If people disobey a rule, the rule is weakened.**

Q. What should people do when they don't agree with a rule?

focal thread: **There are usually several possible alternatives to disobeying a rule that someone doesn't agree with.**

Review the following topics from the first discussion:

- Communities are groups of people.
- The groups of people decide what the rules are going to be in their communities.
- Laws are the rules that communities of people make for themselves.
- Laws, or rules, are meant to protect everyone even though they also limit each person's freedom.

After reviewing the concepts from the first discussion, say, "Let's take a look at one of our communities. We have a community here in our classroom. We are together a good deal of time and we work together." Continue with the following line of questioning:

Q. What are we all trying to do together?
(learn, have fun, do interesting things, make friends, help each other)

Q. Can you think of a rule that we have in our classroom?

Q. Why do we have that rule?

Q. What if I were to take a marker and draw on our wall? Is there a rule about that in our classroom? Why do we have that rule? Could I draw on the wall in the gym? Is it a rule in the gym, too?

Then choose a rule that one of the students named as a classroom rule. Apply the previous questioning so students decide whether that rule applies in the gym, on the playground, at their homes, and why.

Continue questioning:

Q. What do we do when somebody breaks a rule?

Q. How is our reaction different for breaking different rules?

Q. Where can we go to get a rule or law changed?

Q. How do you feel when you see someone break a rule that you follow?

Continue by saying, "There are many different types of courts in the United States. The two largest court systems are the **criminal** and **civil** systems. We're going to be learning about the criminal law and court system. This is the system that is designed to decide who has committed crimes and to punish people for committing crimes."

Q: What if one person is punished for breaking a rule or committing a crime and another person isn't?

Q: Why do we enforce rules or laws?

Q: Suppose one group, Xs, are punished for hitting or hurting people, but another group, Ys, are not. Which group is going to follow the rule? Will the Xs follow the rule if Ys aren't punished? Are the Ys going to follow the rule or law if they aren't punished?

Q: What if the Ys are punished, too, but they are always punished in secret, so that no one else ever sees them punished for breaking the rule?

Present the following hypothetical situation and then discuss the questions that follow.

Let's suppose that there is a group of children waiting in line with one adult at the front of the line. Suppose Child A hits Child B with a backpack. Child B is hurt by this. Child B gets angry and hits Child A back. The adult sees Child B hit Child A. Several of the other kids in line saw Child A hit Child B.

Q: What should the adult do?

Q: What should the other kids do?

Q: Who is responsible, the other kids or the adult or all of them, for making sure that Child A and/or Child B are reprimanded or punished?

Q: Should either one be punished or reprimanded?

Q: If the community is the group of kids, which person, A or B, is a greater threat to the community?

Q: Which one (or both) is more likely to hurt other people in the community?

Q: What if hitting with a backpack hurts people more than hitting them with a hand? Should there be a difference between the reprimands or punishments?

Q: Who is the punishment intended to help? Just the person who got hurt? All of the people in the community?

Explain that in the American criminal court system, two sides are represented. The side that brings charges against someone who did something wrong is called the **prosecution**. The prosecution represents the people of the community, not just the person who got hurt. That is because the community is hurt by anyone who breaks the laws. If someone is allowed to hurt one person, there is a good chance that he or she will hurt other people. And the community has to stop people from hurting other people.

The other side is called the **defense**, because it represents the person who is accused of hurting someone and he or she is defending him or herself. The person accused is called the **defendant**. The defendant might give a reason why he or she had to hurt the other person or might say he or she didn't do it.

Q: Let us go back to children A and B, where Child A hit Child B with a backpack and then Child B hit Child A. Lets say Child B is being charged with hurting Child A. What should Child B say to defend himself?

Q: Is it okay for Child B to hit Child A if Child A hit him first?

Q: What if Child A has hit Child B many times before?

Q: What if Child A has hit, pushed, and said mean things to many other people before?

Q: What if Child A had hit Child B and then pulled his backpack back to hit Child B again?

Q: What if no one saw Child A hit Child B?

Trial Vocabulary

acquit - to prove or to find someone not guilty.

bailiff - an officer (like a sheriff) who is in charge of maintaining order in a court of law.

convict - to prove that someone is guilty.

court - a place where justice is administered.

charge - an accusation that someone has broken the law.

crime - an act or an action that is against the law or a failure to do what the law requires.

criminal - someone who has committed a crime.

cross-examine - to question a witness called by the opposing side.

defendant - a person against whom a charge is brought in a court of law.

defense - pleading of the defendant in answer to charges against him or her.

deliberate - to give something careful thought.

evidence - something that gives proof.

fact - something that happened.

guilty - having done something wrong.

innocent - not guilty of a crime or fault.

judge - an official who can conduct hearings and decide on cases in a court of law.

law - a rule made by a country, state, or town for the people there.

lawyer - a person who represents other people in a court of law.

malicious destruction - intentional destruction of property with the intent of causing another person suffering.

opinion - a belief based on what one thinks or feels rather than on the facts.

plead - to give an answer for charges in court.

testify - to state something under oath.

presumed innocent - the assumption that someone who has been charged with a crime is innocent of that crime until the prosecution proves otherwise.

procedure - a method of doing something in a correct or orderly way.

prosecution - the officials who carry out legal proceedings against someone accused of a crime.

prosecutor - someone who brings charges in court against someone.

reasonable doubt - doubt that is fair or logical; based on facts and reason rather than on opinion or feelings.

testimony - the statement of a witness under oath.

trial - the examination and deciding of a case brought before a court of law.

try - to examine or investigate a case before a court of law.

verdict - the decision made by a jury at the end of a trial.

witness - someone who is called to testify before a court of law.

Vocabulary Match

Match each word with its definition.

_____ acquit

_____ convict

_____ court

_____ crime

_____ criminal

_____ cross-examine

_____ defense

_____ deliberate

_____ evidence

_____ guilty

_____ innocent

_____ law

_____ lawyer

_____ plead

_____ procedure

_____ prosecutor

_____ reasonable doubt

_____ testify

_____ trial

_____ verdict

_____ witness

A. someone who has committed a crime

B. to give an answer for charges in court.

C. pleading of the defendant in answer to charges against him or her

D. the decision made by a jury at the end of a trial

E. having done something wrong

F. a rule made by a country, state, or town for the people there

G. doubt that is fair or logical; based on facts and reason rather than opinion or feelings

H. someone who brings charges in court against someone

I. an act or an action that is against the law or a failure to do what the law requires

J. someone who is called to testify before a court of law

K. to question a witness called by the opposing side

L. to give something careful thought

M. to state something under oath

N. the examination and deciding of a case brought before a court of law

O. something that gives proof

P. to prove or to find someone not guilty

Q. a person who represents other people in a court of law

R. a place where justice is administered

S. not guilty of a crime or fault

T. to prove that someone is guilty

U. a method of doing something in a correct or orderly way

ON TRIAL
The Case of the Big Bad Wolf

Vocabulary

crime

court

defendant

evidence

judge

lawyer

malicious destruction

murder

presumed innocent

prosecution

testimony

trial

witness

We are going to conduct a criminal trial. We will try the Big Bad Wolf for four crimes — the malicious destruction of two houses and the murder of two pigs.

We are going to work with a version of the story that is a combination of several of the stories that you have read about the three pigs and the wolf. Some of the facts in our case, however, are new and not in any story you've read about the Big Bad Wolf. Many of the characters are new. Everybody in the class will play a role in the trial.

A trial is a procedure to decide whether someone has broken the law. A trial is held in a courtroom, also called a court. The trial is conducted by a judge. The judge is an expert in the law and the rules of the court. The judge makes sure that everyone follows the law and the rules of the court. The judge makes sure that the trial is fair.

There are two sides represented in the courtroom – the side that is accusing a person of committing a crime and the side that is defending the accused person. Each side has lawyers that call witnesses to give evidence to prove that the person is guilty or not guilty of the crime.

In a criminal trial, the person accused of committing the crime is called the defendant. He or she is defending himself or herself against the charges. The prosecution is on the other side. The prosecution is part of the government, trying to prove that the defendant committed the crime. The prosecution lawyers are called prosecutors. The defendant also has lawyers called defense attorneys. The defendant is presumed innocent. This means that everyone in the courtroom, especially the judge and jury, must assume that the defendant did not commit the crime; that he or she is innocent. The prosecution has to prove that the accused person is guilty. The defense does not have to prove that the defendant is innocent, but the defense can show evidence that he or she is innocent if they want to.

The prosecution has to call witnesses to the witness stand and ask them questions. The witnesses' answers are called the testimony in the trial. The prosecutors have to give the judge and jury enough evidence (answers from witnesses) to prove that the defendant is guilty beyond a reasonable doubt. That means that there has to be enough evidence that an average person, like one of us, would not have a good reason to think the defendant is innocent.

In our trial, we will be trying the Big Bad Wolf for several crimes. The prosecution is charging Big Bad with two counts of malicious destruction for blowing down two houses. The crime malicious destruction includes two parts – the destroying of property and the intent to destroy. So the prosecutors have to prove beyond a reasonable doubt that Big Bad destroyed each house and that he intended to destroy them. Big Bad is also charged with the murder of two pigs. Murder is the intentional killing of a person by another person. (We will call the wolf and pigs people). The prosecution will have to prove beyond a reasonable doubt that Big Bad killed each pig and that he intended to kill them.

Trial Procedures

Vocabulary

bailiff

charge

cross-examination

defense

lawyer

plead

unanimous

verdict

witness

1. Everyone in the courtroom must act politely and respectfully. Always call the judge "Your Honor" and address the lawyers, witnesses and others as "Mister" or "Miss." Stand when the judge comes in. Be silent in the courtroom unless it is your turn to talk. The judge or one of the lawyers will tell you when it is your turn. Dress nicely in court. Always take time to think before you speak. Always tell the truth.

2. The witnesses, lawyers, and the defendant are seated in the courtroom before the judge comes in and the trial starts. The jury waits outside of the courtroom. The prosecutors sit at one table facing the judge and the defense attorneys and the defendant sit at another table next to the prosecutors, also facing the judge. The witnesses and spectators sit behind the lawyers' tables.

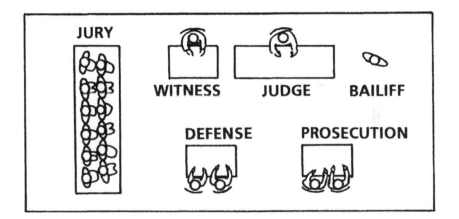

3. The bailiff announces that the judge is coming in and asks everyone to stand up to show respect for the judge, the court, and the law. Everyone is quiet in the courtroom until the judge gives them permission to speak. The bailiff will tell everyone when the trial is about to start by saying:
"All rise. The court is now in session. The honorable Judge _____ (judge's name) is presiding."

4. The judge will then walk in and sit down. The judge will then tell everyone that they may sit down.

5. The judge tells everyone what the trial will be about, asks the defendant whether he or she pleads guilty or not guilty, and then tells the bailiff to bring in the jury. He or she then says,

   "This is the trial of Big Bad Wolf on four charges. The charges are the destruction of Ann's straw house, the murder of Ann, the destruction of Bob's stick house, and the murder of Bob. Mr./Ms. Wolf, how do you plead?"

   Wolf answers, "not guilty," and then the judge says, *"Bailiff, will you please bring in the jury?"*

   The jury will sit down.

6. The judge then asks:

   "Who is representing the people?" The prosecutors stand and give their names.

   "Prosecution, are you ready to proceed?" The prosecutors answer, *"Yes."*

   "Who is representing the defendant?" The defense attorneys stand and give their names.

   "Are you ready to proceed?" The defense attorneys answer, *"Yes."*

7. The judge then asks the lawyers to make their opening statements to the jury. The opening statements are the lawyers' explanations to the jury of the evidence that they will be presenting and why the jury should decide that this side is right. The prosecutor goes first. The defense lawyer goes second.

8. After each side has given an opening statement, the judge will ask if the prosecution is ready to begin calling witnesses.

9. The prosecution calls witnesses first. The prosecuting attorney will call the name of the witness who is supposed to come forward, saying, *"The prosecution calls . . . "* After the prosecution has called all of its witnesses to testify, the defense calls its witnesses.

10. The witness walks forward to the witness stand, which is a chair next to the judge. The witness stands and faces the court. The bailiff swears in each witness, asking the witness if he or she promises to tell the whole truth and then asking to give his or her name.

11. The lawyer who called the witness will ask the witness questions intended to get the witness to give evidence that supports that attorney's side. When that attorney is finished asking questions, he or she says to the judge and witness, *"Thank you, that is all."*

12. The lawyers on the other side then have a chance to ask that witness questions. This is called cross-examination. When the first lawyer, who called the witness is finished, the judge will tell the other side that it may examine the witness.

13. After all of the witnesses have been called, examined and cross-examined, the judge will ask the lawyers if they have any other witnesses. If they do not, the judge will call on the prosecutors to make a closing statement and then on the defense attorneys to do the same. The closing statements should summarize the evidence that has been presented and should make an appeal for the jury to decide for that side.

14. When closing statements are finished, the judge will instruct the jury. The judge will tell them the rules they have to follow when they discuss the case and reach a verdict. He or she will reinforce the principle that the defendant is **innocent until proven guilty** by the prosecution.

15. After the jury has been instructed, the judge will ask the bailiff to take the jury to the jury room. Everyone except the bailiff and jury is then dismissed and will be called back to court when the jury has reached a verdict.

16. When the jury comes back into the courtroom, the judge will ask for the verdict. The judge will say, *"Will the foreman of the jury please stand? Mister/Madame Foreman, have you reached a verdict?"*
The foreman will answer, *"Yes, your honor."*
The judge then says, *"Will the defendant please stand?"* Defendant and defense lawyers stand.
Then the judge says, *"You may read the verdict."*

17. The jury foreman will read the verdict.

18. After the verdict is read, the judge makes sure the verdict is unanimous by saying, *"So say you all?"* to which the entire jury should respond, *"Yes."*

19. Depending on the verdict, the defendant is then told he/she is released or is taken into custody by the bailiff. The judge will end the trial by saying, *"Court is dismissed."*

Bailiff

You are the bailiff in this case. That means that you are the judge's assistant in running the trial and keeping order in the courtroom. You speak several times during the trial. You play a very serious role in the court, because you are a symbol of the honor of the court and of the law. As you carry out your role, speak clearly and strongly.

Opening the Court

At the beginning of the trial you will announce the judge's entrance. When the witnesses and lawyers are in the court and the judge is ready to come in, you will loudly and strongly say, *"All rise,"* meaning that everybody should stand up and be quiet.

Then you will say, *"The first circuit court of (your school) is now in session, the honorable (name of judge) presiding."* The judge will come in.

You will stand next to the judge during the trial. The judge might allow you to sit. The judge will ask you to bring in the jury when everyone is ready. When you are told to do this, go out into the hall and bring the jury into the room.

Swearing In Witnesses

After this, you will speak whenever a witness is called. When the witness is at the witness stand, walk over to him or her and say, *"Do you swear to tell the truth, the whole truth, and nothing but the truth?"*

The witness will answer, *"Yes."*

Then you say, *"Please state your name for the court."* The witness will state his or her name. Then you say, *"Please be seated."*

Being in Charge of the Jury

You will be in charge of the jury when they go into another room to decide on a verdict. At the end of the lawyer's closing statements, the judge will tell you to take the jury out of the court to deliberate. You will lead them out of the room and to the room where they will talk together. Take them into the room and wait nearby. They will come out to tell you when they have reached a verdict. When the jury tells you that they are ready, go in and tell the judge that the jury is ready to give their verdict. The judge will call everybody back into the courtroom. Then he or she will tell you to go and get the jury. You will get the jury and bring them back into the courtroom and have them sit down. Then the judge will talk to them and ask for their verdict.

Ending the Trial

If the defendant is found guilty of any crime, the judge will have you take the defendant into custody. This means that you will go over to the defendant and take him gently but firmly out of the courtroom, as you pretend to take him to jail.

Lawyers

You and the other lawyers will do the most work in this trial. You will also talk the most in court. If you are going to be a lawyer in this case, be certain that you are willing to work hard, in class and at home, and that you are willing to speak in front of the entire court. You will need to take this work very seriously. You will need to read every bit of information that you have received about the trial many times so you know it very well. If you do these things, you will make a good lawyer.

✴ Getting Ready for Trial

Your Legal Team

If you are a lawyer for the prosecution, you have to show that Big Bad is guilty beyond a reasonable doubt. If you are a lawyer for the defense, you will want to show that the prosecution has not proven that Big Bad is guilty. There will be two lawyers on the prosecution side and two lawyers on the side of the defense.

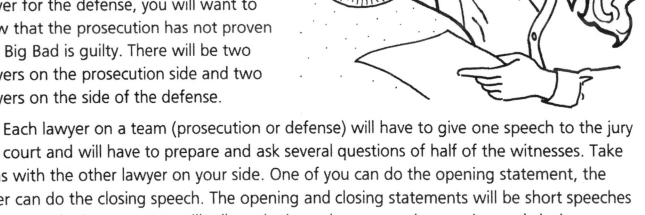

Each lawyer on a team (prosecution or defense) will have to give one speech to the jury and court and will have to prepare and ask several questions of half of the witnesses. Take turns with the other lawyer on your side. One of you can do the opening statement, the other can do the closing speech. The opening and closing statements will be short speeches that you make in court. You will talk to the jury when you make opening and closing statements because you are trying to persuade the jury to reach the verdict that you want.

Planning Questions

You will also be asking the witnesses questions. With your partner, divide up the witnesses so that you take turns asking questions. Remember that in addition to questioning witnesses that you call, you also have to cross-examine the other side's witnesses, so you have to prepare questions for every witness in the trial.

When you ask questions you are trying to get the witness to give answers (testimony) that support your side. Start planning your questions by reading the files for each of the witnesses. Then read each file again, this time underlining the facts that you want the witness to say in court, that is, the facts that help your case. Then talk to your partner (co-counsel). Divide up the witnesses between you, each taking half. Very carefully reread each of the files for the witnesses assigned to you.

Write the questions that will make the witness give the answer that you want to hear in the court. Remember that the jury's verdict will depend upon what they hear in court. They will not know everything that you know. You must get your witnesses to give the evidence that will help your side. Make sure that you know which of the two lawyers on your legal team is responsible for which witnesses and that you have planned the right questions to get the right answers. Ask your co-counsel for advice and help and be sure to help him or her with questions, too. You are a team, and you want to prove your case.

✱ Your Courtroom Procedures

You and your co-counsel will prove your case in three ways. First, you will make an opening statement to the jury to explain what you will prove to them. Second, you will call witnesses to the witness stand and ask them questions. Finally, you will make a final statement to the jury, telling them what evidence you have shown them and asking them to find Big Bad guilty or not guilty.

Your Three Duties

- make an opening statement
- question witnesses
- make a closing statement

Opening Statement

Your first encounter with the jury is your opening statement. Your statement should follow this format:

1. Greet the jurors. Say, *"Good morning,"* or *"Ladies and gentlemen,"* or *"Hello, ladies and gentlemen,"* or something like this.

2. Introduce yourself and your co-counsel. *" I am _____ and this is _____ . We are lawyers representing the people of ___ (your state - prosecution) or the Big Bad Wolf (defense)."*

3. Begin your argument. Before the trial, make a list of the facts you expect your witnesses to give. Tell the jury what you expect them to hear from your witnesses.

   The prosecution might say, *"We will prove to you beyond a reasonable doubt that the Big Bad Wolf destroyed Ann's house and killed Ann and that he destroyed Bob's house and killed Bob. We will have witnesses who will tell you. . ."* (briefly tell them what facts they will hear).

   The defense might say, *"The prosecution will not be able to prove Big Bad Wolf is guilty of any of the charges because he is not guilty. We will have witnesses who will tell you (briefly tell them what facts they will hear)."* List the facts clearly. For instance, *"Little Good Wolf will tell you that. . . "* (then list what he or she will say to convince the jury that your side is right).

Calling and Questioning Witnesses

1. Look at your list of witnesses and call them in order. Say, *"The people (or defense) call Fluff the Lamb."* After the bailiff has sworn in the witness and asked the witness to give his or her name, you can ask questions.

2. Check your list of facts next to each name and ask each witness questions that will make him or her give the answers that you want. For example, *"Where were you on Saturday, April 13 in the afternoon?"* or *"What did you see that afternoon?"* and so on. Check off your questions as you finish them.

3. After you have asked your questions, check with your partner (co-counsel) and refer to the list of facts to make sure you have asked the witness everything that you need to. When you have finished asking questions of the witness, tell the judge that you are done.

4. The judge will then tell the opposing lawyers that they may cross-examine the witness. The other side's lawyer will then ask the witness questions.

Closing Statement

Reread the preceding section describing the opening statement. The closing statement is very much like the opening statement, except that the closing is a speech that you make to the jury in which you describe what you have proven during the trial.

Start your closing by saying that your have proven your case. Prosecutors can say, *"The Big Bad Wolf is guilty of destroying two houses and killing two pigs,"* or *"There is no reasonable doubt that the Big Bad Wolf has committed these crimes,"* or *"The evidence has proven that the Big Bad Wolf committed four terrible crimes."* The defense attorneys can say, *"There is not enough evidence to prove that the Big Bad Wolf committed these crimes,"* or *"The prosecution has not proven its case, so you must acquit the Big Bad Wolf."* You do not have to use these exact sentences.

Be sure to talk to the jury convincingly. You must tell the jury that your side is right. Tell them which verdict they should reach. Then list the evidence that you have shown in court that supports that verdict. Tell the jury about each witness' testimony and why it supports the verdict you want. After you have listed all of the evidence that you want the jury to remember, tell them again that this evidence proves (prosecution) or hasn't proven (defense) that the Big Bad Wolf is guilty of each of the crimes. Finish your closing statement by telling the jurors which verdict they should reach: guilty for the prosecution or not guilty for the defense.

You will be called as a witness in the trial. The bailiff will ask you to promise to tell the truth and you must promise to do so. The truth is the information given below. It is very important that you read this information many times before the trial and that you know it well. After you have studied this material, take this sheet home and have a family member ask you lots of questions from it. Answer the questions based only on the information given here. When you are asked a question, in court or at home, to which you do not know the answer, you should answer, "I don't know." Do not make up any information.

If your class has news reporters, you may decide whether you want to talk to the reporters and answer their questions or not. The choice is yours.

These Are Your Facts

♦ You received a phone call late in the afternoon on Saturday, April 13 from someone saying that two houses had just been destroyed near the woods. The caller told you to come right away to the new neighborhood near the woods because he/she was worried. The caller said that he/she could not find the owner.

♦ You went to the new neighborhood with your deputy and found a group of animals gathered around a pile of straw and a pile of sticks. You investigated the area to find out what had happened.

♦ You found a pile of straw that looked very strange. It was not a pile in the shape of a cone or a pyramid, like someone would have made if they had piled up the straw. Instead the pile looked tipped over, as though someone had pushed it or the wind had blown it in one direction. You found this very unusual. It was not windy that day. There had not been any storms that would have brought a tornado or wind gust that might have blown over the house.

♦ There was a pile of sticks next to the pile of straw. It also looked like wind had blown it down or someone had pushed it over.

♦ You began talking to some of the animals standing around the piles. You wrote down everything they said so you could make your police report.

♦ You talked to a horse named Quarter. Quarter told you that a pig named Ann lived in the straw house. Quarter lived next to Ann but had not seen her that day. Quarter said that he/she had not seen anything or anyone that might have caused the house to fall down. Quarter had, however, heard someone yelling, "Little pig, little pig, let me come in." Then Quarter heard the same voice say, "Then I'll huff and I'll puff and I'll blow your house in." Quarter went outside and Ann's house was destroyed. Next door to Ann's house, her brother Bob's stick house was also gone, just a pile of sticks. Quarter said it had not been windy at all, but Quarter had seen wolves in the area about a week earlier.

♦ You looked around for the two missing pigs, but you haven't found them yet. You haven't, however, found any evidence that they were eaten, either.

You will be called as a witness in the trial. The bailiff will ask you to promise to tell the truth and you must promise to do so. The truth is the information given below. It is very important that you read this information many times before the trial and that you know it well. After you have studied this material, take this sheet home and have a family member ask you lots of questions from it. Answer the questions based only on the information given here. When you are asked a question, in court or at home, to which you do not know the answer, you should answer, "I don't know." Do not make up any information.

If your class has news reporters, you may decide whether you want to talk to the reporters and answer their questions or not. The choice is yours.

These Are Your Facts

♦ You are the deputy for the town. You were in the sheriff's office when the sheriff received a phone call and told you that you had to go to the scene of a crime.

♦ You went to the new neighborhood near the woods where you saw a group of animals and two piles. There was a pile of straw and a pile of sticks. The sheriff asked you to talk to some witnesses and write down what they told you.

♦ You talked to the animal who had called to report the event. The animal was named Quack, a very nervous goose who lived across the street from Ann's and Bob's houses. Quack had seen Ann that morning and everything had seemed fine. Quack was sure that Ann had been at home when the house was ruined. Through the front window of Quack's house, Quack had seen Ann run into the straw house. Quack had seen a wolf going toward Ann's house. A few minutes later, Quack saw that Ann's and Bob's houses had been destroyed. Ann and Bob were missing.

♦ You then talked to Fluff, the lamb who lived next to Bob's house. Fluff had seen a wolf outside of Bob's house, yelling about blowing his house in. Then Fluff saw the wolf blow the house down. When the house fell down, Fluff saw that Ann's house was already in a shambles. Fluff saw the wolf run toward Bob's ruined house. Fluff can't remember anything after that because the lamb fainted from fright. Fluff told you that all wolves should be in prison but couldn't give you a clear description of the wolf.

You will be called as a witness in the trial. The bailiff will ask you to promise to tell the truth and you must promise to do so. The truth is the information given below. It is very important that you read this information many times before the trial and that you know it well. After you have studied this material, take home this sheet and have a family member ask you lots of questions from it. Answer the questions based only on the information given here. When you are asked a question, in court or at home, to which you do not know the answer, you should answer, "I don't know." Do not make up any information.

If your class has news reporters, you may decide whether you want to talk to the reporters and answer their questions or not. The choice is yours.

These Are Your Facts

♦ You were a neighbor of Ann, the pig whose straw house was destroyed. You live in a strong stable with another horse, Shadow.

♦ You were home on Saturday, April 13, but you had not seen Ann that day. You had been in the pasture most of the day. After you came home, you heard yelling outside. It was coming from the direction of Ann's house. You didn't look outside. You hid. The voice sounded loud and scary. It said, "Little pig, little pig, let me come in!" Then you heard the voice say, "Then I'll huff and I'll puff and I'll blow your house in." You heard a big wind, even though it hadn't been windy all day. You heard a pig squeal and then the sound of someone running away.

♦ When you came out of your stable, you saw Ann's house in shambles, just a pile of straw. It looked as though it had been blown over. You didn't see anyone. Bob's house was also destroyed. You haven't seen Ann or Bob since all of this happened.

♦ About a week ago you had seen wolves around the neighborhood. You had seen a wolf lurking around the houses just before dawn a few days ago. You had also seen a wolf sneaking around the edge of the woods next to the neighborhood twice at night last week. You didn't see the wolves very well. One of them could have been the defendant, Big Bad, but you're not sure.

You will be called as a witness in the trial. The bailiff will ask you to promise to tell the truth and you must promise to do so. The truth is the information given below. It is very important that you read this information many times before the trial and that you know it well. After you have studied this material, take home this sheet and have a family member ask you lots of questions from it. Answer the questions based only on the information given here. When you are asked a question, in court or at home, to which you do not know the answer, you should answer, "I don't know." Do not make up any information.

If your class has news reporters, you may decide whether you want to talk to the reporters and answer their questions or not. The choice is yours.

These Are Your Facts

♦ You lived next to Bob. You were at home on Saturday, April 13. You were in your house when you heard a loud noise outside. You looked outside and saw a wolf yelling at Bob's house. The wolf said, "Little pig, little pig, let me come in."

♦ You heard Bob's voice answer, "Not by the hair of my chinny chin chin."

♦ The wolf said, "Then I'll huff and I'll puff and I'll blow your house in."

♦ Then you saw the wolf suck in a lot of air and blow the house down. When it fell down, you saw that Ann's straw house was also destroyed. You heard a pig squealing.

♦ Then you felt very faint. You can't remember seeing anything else until you woke up on the floor of your house later. When you woke up, there were animals in the street yelling and standing around the two destroyed houses.

♦ You are not sure that Big Bad is the same wolf you saw outside of Bob's house. You hate wolves and think they should all be prison if they won't stay in the woods. You think there are far too many wolves in this area. You have seen them lurking about many times. You can't tell one wolf from another.

You will be called as a witness in the trial. The bailiff will ask you to promise to tell the truth and you must promise to do so. The truth is the information given below. It is very important that you read this information many times before the trial and that you know it well. After you have studied this material, take this sheet home and have a family member ask you lots of questions from it. Answer the questions based only on the information given here. When you are asked a question, in court or at home, to which you do not know the answer, you should answer, "I don't know." Do not make up any information.

If your class has news reporters, you may decide whether you want to talk to the reporters and answer their questions or not. The choice is yours.

These Are Your Facts

◆ You live across the street from Ann and Bob.

◆ You were at home on the afternoon of Saturday, April 13. You saw Ann that morning. That afternoon you were in your backyard playing soccer with your goslings. You saw a wolf sneaking along the edge of the woods behind your house. You quickly called the goslings to come into the house immediately, and you all flew and waddled inside as fast as you could.

◆ When you got inside, you got all of the goslings into a safe place and went to the window to watch the wolf. You saw the wolf moving very slowly through the woods, hiding behind trees. The wolf was watching everything carefully.

◆ When the wolf got to the edge of your yard, the wolf dashed to the street. You couldn't see the wolf out of the window anymore, so you went to check on the goslings to make sure they were still safe. As you ran through the house, you looked out your front window. You saw Ann running into her house.

◆ Your goslings were quacking and squawking so you couldn't hear anything, but after a while you went to check the front window. You saw that Ann and Bob's houses were destroyed.

◆ You called the sheriff. You haven't seen Ann and Bob since April 13.

◆ You are certain that the wolf you saw in your yard that afternoon was the defendant, Big Bad Wolf.

You will be called as a witness in the trial. The bailiff will ask you to promise to tell the truth and you must promise to do so. The truth is the information given below. It is very important that you read this information many times before the trial and that you know it well. After you have studied this material, take home the sheet and have a family member ask you lots of questions from it. Answer the questions based only on the information given here. When you are asked a question, in court or at home, to which you do not know the answer, you should answer, "I don't know." Do not make up any information

If your class has news reporters, you may decide whether you want to talk to the reporters and answer their questions or not. The choice is yours.

These Are Your Facts

- ◆ You were a friend of Ann and Bob. You were also the architect for their houses. You helped them design each of their houses.

- ◆ You are a licensed architect who has been designing and building houses for over three years. You went to architecture school and got straight A's. You have won two awards for your architecture. You are famous for your work.

- ◆ You drew the plans for both Ann's and Bob's houses. The plans were for big strong houses. In your opinion, the houses you designed could not fall down if they were built exactly as you designed them.

- ◆ You did not help to build the houses, though. Ann built her house by herself, with some help from some of the neighborhood mice. You never work with mice, because you can be dangerous near lunch time when mice are around. Ann and the mice built the house out of straw. You have never built a house out of straw, so you don't know how strong it would be.

- ◆ Bob's house was made out of sticks, so you think it should have been stronger than a house made out of straw. Of course, it depends on what Bob used to keep the sticks together. Nails would make the house stronger than glue or tape. You don't know what Bob used, but a stick house could be pretty strong.

You will be called as a witness in the trial. The bailiff will ask you to promise to tell the truth and you must promise to do so. The truth is the information given below. It is very important that you read this information many times before the trial and that you know it well. After you have studied this material, take this sheet home and have a family member ask you lots of questions from it. Answer the questions based only on the information given here. When you are asked a question, in court or at home, to which you do not know the answer, you should answer, "I don't know." Do not make up any information.

If your class has news reporters, **do not talk to the reporters and do not answer any of their questions.**

These Are Your Facts

♦ You are a teacher at the local college. You teach animal science and are an expert on wolves.

♦ You do not know Ann, Bob, or Big Bad Wolf.

♦ You have studied wolves a lot. You are famous throughout America as a wolf expert. You were hired by the United States government when there were problems with wolves at the White House.

♦ Your study of wolves has taught you many things. First, wolves eat animals. They eat the meatiest animals that they can find. It is common for wolves to eat pigs and sheep. Wolves are very clever and cunning hunters. One wolf can eat a whole pig very quickly. Usually a wolf will not kill another pig after just eating a whole pig, but a wolf might catch another pig and take it into the woods to eat later or to share with its pack or family. In early spring wolves are usually desperate and hungry.

♦ The bigger the wolf, the more it can eat. In your opinion, Big Bad Wolf is a very large wolf, capable of eating a whole pig quickly.

♦ Even a very large wolf will not kill unless it is hungry. If a wolf is starving, it will eat much more than usual.

You will be called as a witness in the trial. The bailiff will ask you to promise to tell the truth and you must promise to do so. The truth is the information given below. It is very important that you read this information many times before the trial and that you know it well. After you have studied this material, take this sheet home and have a family member ask you lots of questions from it. Answer the questions based only on the information given here. When you are asked a question, in court or at home, to which you do not know the answer, you should answer, "I don't know." Do not make up any information.

If your class has news reporters, you may decide whether you want to talk to the reporters and answer their questions or not. The choice is yours.

These Are Your Facts

♦ You are a friend of Big Bad Wolf. You see each other every day because you live in the same woods. You get along well with your friend. The only time that you have fought is when you have argued about food. You believe that wolves should stay out of the towns and farm areas, because if you and other wolves kill people and animals in the towns and farms, the residents might get upset and start killing wolves. You believe that there is enough food in the woods for you and the other wolves.

♦ You were with your friend, Big Bad, on Saturday, April 13. You and Big Bad were sharing a squirrel in the woods that morning, both of you talking and having a good time. Big was in a good mood. The hunting had been very good in the woods recently. In the past few weeks, there were a lot of small animals in the woods. You were with Big Bad for the morning, but you don't know where he was that afternoon.

♦ Most of the other animals don't like you and the other wolves. They are rude to you and often leave when you walk down the street or come into a park. You think that the other animals blame you and the other wolves every time something goes wrong. Once you were accused of taking a couple of lambs, but they were later found. Once one of your wolf friends was accused of taking chickens that were later found in the barn.

♦ You do not think Big Bad Wolf hurt the two pigs or blew down their houses. You think that the pigs built very bad houses that could have fallen down on their own, or the poorly-made houses could have been knocked down easily if some goats or cows had bumped into them. You think the pigs were ashamed that their houses fell down, so they just moved to another town. You think everybody is blaming a wolf for this unfortunate accident because everybody always picks on wolves.

You will be called as a witness in the trial. The bailiff will ask you to promise to tell the truth and you must promise to do so. The truth is the information given below. It is very important that you read this information many times before the trial and that you know it well. After you have studied this material, take this sheet home and have a family member ask you lots of questions from it. Answer the questions based only on the information given here. When you are asked a question, in court or at home, to which you do not know the answer, you should answer, "I don't know." Do not make up any information.

If your class has news reporters, you may decide whether you want to talk to the reporters and answer their questions or not. The choice is yours.

These Are Your Facts

♦ You are Big Bad Wolf's doctor, and you live in the woods near him.

♦ Big Bad Wolf had a doctor's appointment with you at the end of March for his annual checkup.

♦ At his last check up, Big Bad was in good shape for a wolf of his age. Of course, all of the animals in the woods are a little thin and weak in the early spring because the hunting is not good in the winter. Some of the animals are starving by the end of March. Big Bad Wolf, however, was in good shape; certainly not starving, but maybe unusually hungry. You don't know what the hunting was like that winter because you were hibernating until the middle of March.

♦ Big Bad Wolf is a stronger and bigger wolf than the average wolf. He is about five years old and is much stronger than very old wolves or baby wolves. He has a full set of good teeth and well-developed muscles. Compared to other wolves, he has very large, strong lungs.

You will be called as a witness in the trial. The bailiff will ask you to promise to tell the truth and you must promise to do so. The truth is the information given below. It is very important that you read this information many times before the trial and that you know it well. After you have studied this material, take this sheet home and have a family member ask you lots of questions from it. Answer the questions based only on the information given here. When you are asked a question, in court or at home, to which you do not know the answer, you should answer, "I don't know." Do not make up any information.

If your class has news reporters, **do not talk to the reporters and do not answer any of their questions.**

These Are Your Facts

♦ You are a beaver and an expert in house building. You have been building houses all of your life.

♦ You build houses out of sticks and small trees. You used straw to build your first house and it did not work well. You found that straw got mushy in water and that water currents and wind easily destroyed the straw areas of the first house you built. You had to repair the straw area of that house with sticks and mud. In your opinion, a straw house can fall down easily in a light wind, if someone bumps into it, or can even fall down all on its own.

♦ In your experience, sticks can make a very strong house, but the key to making a strong stick house is the material you use to put the sticks together. When you heard there was a pig building a house out of sticks, you went over to look at it. You were disgusted. The house was definitely not put together with mud. It looked as though the stick house had been put together with tape. There were little shiny strips at the corners. In your experience, tape will not hold a stick house together because the tape comes loose when it gets wet. Also, after awhile, tape loses its stickiness. In your opinion, a stick house made with tape will be just as fragile as a straw house. It could easily be blown down with an average wind. It could also easily fall over if someone bumped into it.

♦ The stick house was also made with very small sticks, not the large sticks and small trees that you use. None of the other beavers use such little sticks. You certainly never used such little sticks.

♦ In your opinion, either one of the houses (Ann's straw house or Bob's stick house) could have fallen down easily if there was a light wind or if someone bumped into either one of them.

You will be called as a witness in the trial. The bailiff will ask you to promise to tell the truth and you must promise to do so. The truth is the information given below. It is very important that you read this information many times before the trial and that you know it well. After you have studied this material, take this sheet home and have a family member ask you lots of questions from it. Answer the questions based only on the information given here. When you are asked a question, in court or at home, to which you do not know the answer, you should answer, "I don't know." Do not make up any information.

If your class has news reporters, you may decide whether you want to talk to the reporters and answer their questions or not. The choice is yours.

These Are Your Facts

♦ You are a pig who lives in the neighborhood that Ann and Bob lived in. You live in one of the first houses built in the neighborhood. When you first moved into your house, there were many wolves in the area. You have seen lots of wolves in the past few years and by now you know most of the remaining wolves by sight.

♦ You were walking in the neighborhood on the afternoon of Saturday, April 13. As you were passing the corner of the street where Ann and Bob lived, you looked down their street. You saw a wolf standing on the sidewalk in front of Ann's and Bob's houses. You saw the wolf blow down Ann's straw house and you ran back to your house as fast as you could. You went home to make sure your piglets were safe.

♦ You are certain that the wolf that you saw blowing down Ann's house was not Big Bad Wolf. The markings on the wolf's face were different than Big Bad's markings. The wolf was about the same size as Big Bad and had about the same color on its body, but the face was different, you are sure.

♦ You were far away, about 100 yards, from the wolf that you saw blowing down the house. It was late afternoon so there were shadows, but it was still light outside.

♦ You have very good eyesight.

You will be called as a witness in the trial. The bailiff will ask you to promise to tell the truth and you must promise to do so. The truth is the information given below. It is very important that you read this information many times before the trial and that you know it well. After you have studied this material, take this sheet home and have a family member ask you lots of questions from it. Answer the questions based only on the information given here. When you are asked a question, in court or at home, to which you do not know the answer, you should answer, "I don't know." Do not make anything up.

If your class has news reporters, **do not talk to the reporters and do not answer any of their questions**.

These Are Your Facts

♦ You are Big Bad Wolf's cousin. You know Big Bad very well. You do not think Big Bad destroyed the houses or killed the pigs.

♦ You saw Big Bad the day before the houses were destroyed. He seemed well-fed, considering what time of year it was. You and several of the wolves in the pack had been worried about the other animals' blaming the wolves whenever something goes wrong.

♦ You have been to the neighborhood where Ann and Bob lived many times. You knew Ann and Bob liked to have the animals from the neighborhood over to their yards to play soccer. You've seen the animals playing soccer there many times, and you think that someone knocked the houses down when they were playing soccer.

♦ You remember seeing Ann repairing her house many times. In your opinion, it was not a sturdy house at all.

Jurors' Instructions

Your Role

You are a member of the jury. Your job in this trial is the most important job, though you might not get as much attention as some of the other people in the trial. Your job is a quiet job, until the end. Your decision will be very important to everyone involved in the trial and no one can change your decision.

In order to do your job well and reach a fair decision, you must listen very carefully to everything that happens during the trial. You should take notes. After all the evidence has been presented, you must think carefully and fairly and decide whether Big Bad is guilty or not guilty. The Big Bad Wolf is innocent unless the prosecution proves that he is guilty beyond a reasonable doubt.

The Charges

You will decide whether Big Bad Wolf is guilty or not guilty of four separate crimes. The crimes he has been charged with are:

- the destruction of Ann's straw house
- the murder of Ann
- the destruction of Bob's stick house
- the murder of Bob.

Deliberating

At the end of the presentation of evidence and lawyers' statements, the bailiff will take you into another room to deliberate. You will talk to each other and come to decisions on the charges or crimes. When you get into the room, elect a jury foreman. Your jury foreman will be the person who will read your verdicts to the court.

You will decide whether Big Bad is guilty of each of these crimes separately. You might find Big Bad guilty of some of the crimes and not of others, of all of the crimes, or of none of the crimes. You might want to talk about all of the crimes together or talk about each one separately. But, whichever way you start, you have to finish by answering "guilty" or "not guilty" for each separate charge.

It is important that all of you agree on your decision (verdict) for each charge or crime. If you cannot agree, you have to keep talking to each other until you all agree. If you do not agree, talk it over and try to use logic and evidence to convince the people who disagree with you. **You must come to a decision.** If you cannot agree on a verdict, the trial will be declared a mistrial. This is the worst possible ending.

Your Verdict

For each charge, you have to decide whether the prosecution has proven that Big Bad is guilty **beyond a reasonable doubt**. There will be evidence that makes you think Big Bad committed each crime and there will be evidence that makes you think Big Bad did not. Remember that Big Bad is presumed innocent until proven guilty. Then think about all of the evidence that you have heard. Has the prosecution proved to you that Big Bad committed each of these crimes? If you think so, but you have some doubt, think about whether your doubt is reasonable. Is there a pretty good reason to think he's not guilty? Is it a silly reason? Did the prosecutors fail to prove that it was him? Is it logical that it wasn't Big Bad or that the crime didn't happen?

As a jury you have to reach a decision together. Be fair and respectful to all of the witnesses and to your fellow jurors. Listen to their ideas and think carefully about what they've said. Remember that you are the jury; you are a team.

When you've decided about each charge, tell the bailiff. The bailiff will tell the judge and then tell you when you will announce your verdict.

A Note About Reporters

If your class has news reporters, **do not talk to reporters and do not answer any of their questions.**

News Reporter Instructions

You are a reporter for the local newspaper. Your job is to learn about what is happening in the local government and report that information to the public. In playing your role, you will question people involved in the trial. You will be very busy during this class project. There are four basic parts to your job.

1. First, think about what things the public should know about the trial. Often reporters ask the questions who, what, where, when, how, and why.

2. Think about how you can answer these questions for the public. For example, to answer the question "who?," you might need to find out who was involved in the destruction of the houses and the disappearance of the pigs, who saw something, who was hurt, who is involved in the trial, who are the lawyers, or who is the judge. Decide what information you need to get in order to report all the facts of this case. Make a list of questions you will ask each person. Interview the the trial participants to get the information you need.

3. Then write an article before the trial, giving the information that you learned from the participants.

4. Attend the trial and take notes about everything that happens. After the verdict has been announced, write an article about the trial and its outcome.

After the Trial

What Happened? How did it Happen? Why?

When you answer these questions, remember that all actors had a sheet of information that told them what to say. When you talk about the actions of the people in the trial, you are not necessarily talking about the students in your class. You are talking about the roles they played. Also understand that your classmates are not necessarily criticizing you if they criticize the role you played. Think about what you and other actors did in the trial as you answer these questions.

Trial and Verdict

♦ What was the verdict in the trial?

♦ Did you agree with the verdict?

♦ Whether you agreed or not, do you think that the verdict was fair?

♦ Why do you think the jury came to that decision?

♦ What would you have changed about the trial?

♦ What was the most important evidence in the trial?

♦ Did that evidence influence the jury?

♦ Was the trial fair to the Big Bad Wolf?

♦ If it was, what parts of the trial made it fair?

♦ If not, what could have been changed to make it more fair?

♦ Did the lawyers have too much control of the trial or not enough control?

News Reports

If your class had reporters, answer these questions:

♦ Did you read the news story before the trial?

♦ Did the news story accurately give all of the facts in the trial?

♦ Did the news story change the way you felt about the trial?

♦ Did the news story change your opinion about whether the Big Bad Wolf was guilty?

Roles

♦ If you did another trial in class, what role would you want the next time?

♦ Why would you want that role?

Roles, continued

Answer the question that applies to the role you played:

Lawyers

♦ What would you have done differently?

♦ Did each of the witnesses answer the way you expected them to?

♦ Did each of the witnesses answer the way that you wanted them to?

♦ What was the hardest part of the trial for you?

Witnesses

♦ Did you always understand the questions you were asked?

♦ Was there anything that you knew that you were not asked about?

♦ Would that evidence have been important?

♦ Would that evidence have changed the verdict?

Jurors

♦ Were you satisfied with the verdict?

♦ Do you think that the prosecution and defense made the evidence clear to you?

♦ Did you understand all of the witnesses?

♦ What happened during deliberations?

♦ Did you have enough time to deliberate?

♦ Did everyone on the jury agree on a verdict when you first started deliberations?

♦ If not, what happened in the jury room to make some of the people change their minds?

♦ Did the jury members compromise with each other?

Reporters

♦ Was it easy for you to get information for your story before the trial?

♦ Were there persons involved in the case who would not speak to you?

♦ Was it hard to give a fair story when not everyone would talk to you?

♦ Did you have any opinions about the trial?

♦ Did you put your opinions into your news stories?

Bailiff

♦ What was the hardest part of the trial for you?

♦ Did everyone in the courtroom listen to what you said?

Answers

Vocabulary Match - page 15

acquit - P

convict - T

court - R

crime - I

criminal - A

cross-examine - K

defense - C

deliberate - L

evidence - O

guilty - E

innocent - S

law - F

lawyer - Q

plead- B

procedure - U

prosecutor - H

reasonable doubt - G

testify - M

trial - N

verdict - D

witness - J